JOHN ALDEN CARPENTER

SEA DRIFT

FOR ORCHESTRA

ED-3910

ISBN 978-0-7935-3610-8

G. SCHIRMER, Inc.

DISTRIBUTED BY
HAL•LEONARD®
CORPORATION
7777 W. BLUEMOUND RD. P.O. BOX 13819 MILWAUKEE, WI 53213

I have often found, in the case of my compositions, that the germ of an idea may become implanted and then lie dormant for a long period only to be stirred into active life, after perhaps a considerable interval, by influences outside myself and not always recognizable.

Away back around 1915, I experienced my first acute Whitman excitement, and for some time, then, I studied the problem of setting to music in vocal form excerpts from some of the "Sea-Drift" poems. These experiments I could not bring to any result that satisfied me, and I dropped the project.

In February of last year [1933], under the influence of the blue Mediterranean at Eze village, I took up the old problem again, and abandoned any attempt to make a literal setting of the Whitman verses in a vocal work. I tried to make a composite orchestral record of the imprint upon me of these poems. My hope is that the music makes sense, just as music, with perhaps a special meaning for those who love Whitman. My work represents an effort to transcribe my impressions derived from these magnificent poems.

JOHN ALDEN CARPENTER

(in a letter to Lawrence Gilman of the New York Herald Tribune)

This edition is the first publication of the revised version dated 1942.

recordings: New World Records (NW-321-2)
Julius Hegyi and the Albany Symphony

AS Disc (AS 546) Artur Rodzinsky
and the New York Philharmonic
(live premiere recording, 1944)

Performance material is available on rental from the publisher.

INSTRUMENTATION

Piccolo
2 Flutes
2 Oboes
English Horn
2 Clarinets in B♭
2 Bassoons

4 Horns in F
3 Trumpets in B♭
3 Trombones
Tuba

Timpani
Percussion: Glockenspiel, Vibraphone (Deagan no. 145),
   Chimes (low B♭), Cymbals, Gong, Bass Drum

Harp
Celesta
Piano

Strings

duration: ca. 12 minutes

"This music derives its title, and has sought inspiration from the noble sea poems of Walt Whitman."

Performance material is available on rental from the publisher.

SEA DRIFT

John Alden Carpenter
(1933, revised 1942)

Lento tranquillo
♩ = 80

poco accel.

Piccolo

Fl's I II

Obs. I II

E.H.

Cls. B♭ I II

Bsns. I II

Horns F I II

III IV

Tpts I II III

Trbs

Tuba

Timp. — Low D solo — *pp* — *ppp* — *pp* — *pp* — *poco accel.*

Cymb. — soft sticks — *ppp* — *pp* — *pp*

Celesta

Harp

Lento tranquillo
♩ = 80

V. I°

V. II°

Viola — molto legato e espr. — *p*

Celli — *p*

Bassi — *pp*

+Note: *A flexible eighth-note beat is recommended.*

6

11
a tempo
rall molto
a tempo
(♩= 72)
Fl. I° solo
rall. poco
Fl.
Ob.
Cl.
Cl. I°
Horn
I°
solo
pp sopr.
Harp
divi
unis
solo
pizz
arco

Note: ⌢ = short pause,
not a prolonged hold.

♩= 88
rall
♩= 72
Fl. I° solo
accel.
a tempo
Fl.
Ob.
Cls
Bas
Horn
Cymb
Harp
f espr.
agitato
Obs a 2
Soli
16
(In 5)
(In 3)
divi
unis trem.
trem.
pizz
soli
accel.
a tempo
animando molto
♩= 108
a 2
Horns
espr.
arco

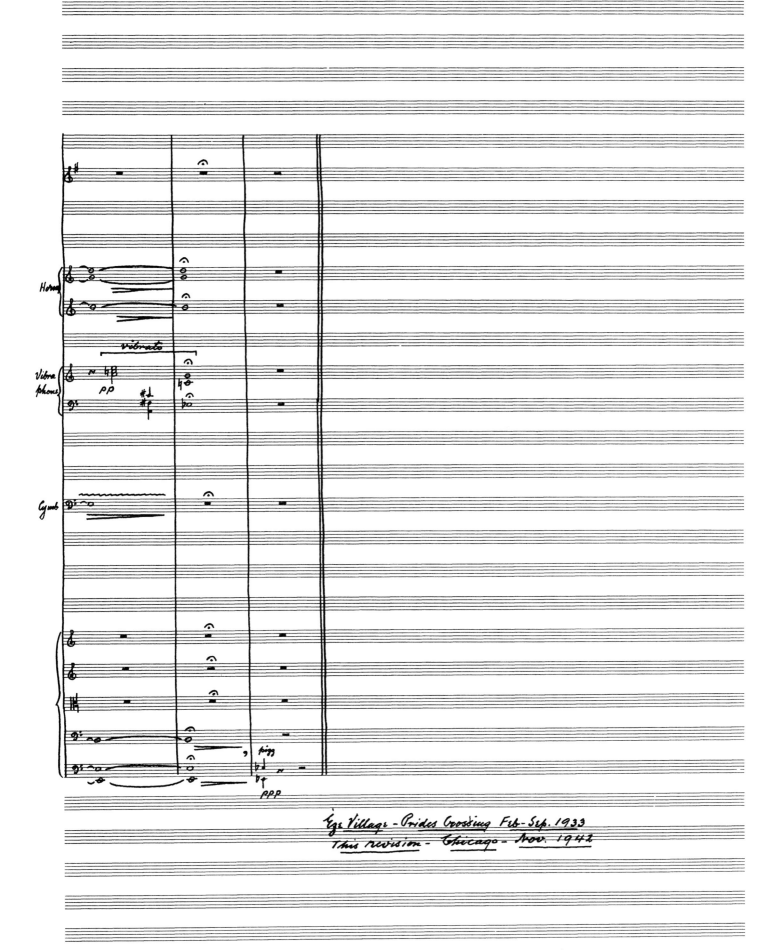